W9-BAL-532

Shakespeare's Garden

Illustrated by
Nancy Shumaker Pallan

Cedco Publishing · San Rafael, California

0-7683-2150-6

Illustrations by Nancy Shumaker Pallan
Art copyright © 1999 Nancy Shumaker Pallan
All rights reserved.

Published in 2000 by Cedco Publishing Company
100 Pelican Way, San Rafael, California 94901.
For a free catalog of other Cedco® products,
please write to the address above, or
visit our website: www.cedco.com

Book and Jacket design by Teena Gores

Printed in Hong Kong

3 5 7 9 10 8 6 4 2

No part of this book may be reproduced
in any manner whatsoever without written
permission except in the case of reprints
in the context of reviews.

To gild refined gold,
to paint the lily...

King John IV, 2

When daffodils
    begin to peer...
Why, then comes in
    the sweet o' the year.

The Winter's Tale IV, 3

What's in a name?
that which we call a rose,
By any other name
would smell as sweet.

Romeo and Juliet II, 2

There's rosemary,
that's for
remembrance ...

Hamlet IV, 5

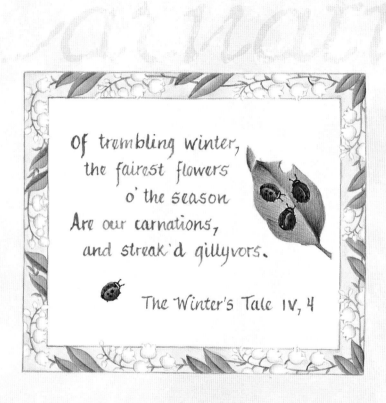

Of trembling winter,
the fairest flowers
o' the season
Are our carnations,
and streak'd gillyvors.

The Winter's Tale IV, 4

When daisies pied
and violets blue ...

Do paint the meadows
with delight.

Love's Labour's Lost V, 2

What sayest thou,
my fair
flower-de-luce?

Henry V v, 2

Mercutio:
   Nay, I am the very
   pink of courtesy.
Romeo:
   Pink for flower.

Romeo and Juliet 11,4

I must have
saffron to colour
the warden pies...

The Winter's Tale IV, 3

There's fennel for you,
and columbines.

Hamlet IV, 5

And there is pansies,
that's for thoughts.

Hamlet IV, 5

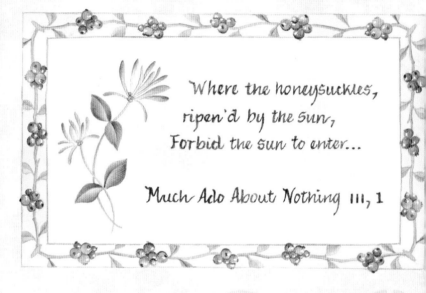

Where the honeysuckles,
ripen'd by the sun,
Forbid the sun to enter...

Much Ado About Nothing III, 1

...I think the king
is but a man,
as I am ;
the violet
smells to him
as it doth to me...

Henry V IV, 1

The flower that's
like your face,
pale primrose ...

Cymbeline IV, 2

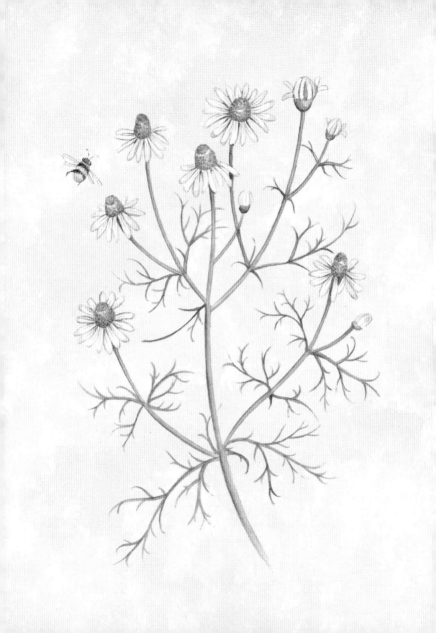